# Exploring Our World

# Tropical Forests

# Terry Jennings

Marshall Cavendish

**The editors gratefully thank the staff of the Havenwoods Forest Preserve of the Wisconsin Department of Natural Resources, Milwaukee, for their technical assistance, use of resource materials, and enthusiastic cooperation in the development of *Exploring Our World.***

**Library of Congress Cataloging-in-Publication Data**
Jennings, Terry J.
   Tropical forests.
   (Exploring our world)
   Bibliography: p.
   Includes index.
   Summary: Discusses tropical forests and their effect on the plants, animals, and humans interacting with them.
   1. Anthropo-geography--Tropics--Juvenile literature.  2.  Forests and forestry--Tropics--Juvenile literature.  3.  Forest ecology--Tropics--Juvenile literature.  4.  Rain forests--Juvenile literature.  [1. Rain forests. 2. Rain forest ecology.  3.  Tropics.  4.  Ecology]  I. Title.  II. Series:  Exploring our world (Freeport, N.Y.)
GF54.5.J465  1987        910'.0913          87-24278
ISBN 0-86307-821-4

This North American edition first published in 1987 by

Marshall Cavendish Corporation
147 West Merrick Road
Freeport, NY 11520

This US edition copyright © 1987.  First published in the United Kingdom by Oxford University Press in 1986 under the title **The Young Geographer Investigates: Tropical Forests** by Oxford University Press.

This format conceived, designed, and produced by Gareth Stevens Publishing, Milwaukee.

Typeset by Web Tech, Milwaukee.
Format and design: Laurie Bishop and Laurie Shock.
Series editors: MaryLee Knowlton and Rhoda Sherwood.
Technical consultant: Robert Brinkmann, Department of Geography, the University of Wisconsin-Milwaukee.

1 2 3 4 5 6 7 8 9  92 91 90 89 88 87

*The publishers would like to thank the following for permission to use transparencies:*

Aspect Picture Library p. 19 (top and bottom), p. 22, p. 26 (bottom right), p. 30 (top right), p. 31 (bottom right), p. 33 (top right); Bruce Coleman Ltd./Frith p.5 (left); Coleman/Schultz p. 5 (top right); Coleman/Marigo p. 5 (bottom right); Coleman/Compost p. 11 (left), p. 14 (inset); Coleman/Calhoun p. 16 (bottom); Coleman/Burton p. 40; Coleman/Hinchcliffe p. 39; Coleman/Crichton p. 38; Coleman/Jackson p. 21 (right); Sally and Richard Greenhill p. 28 (top); Susan Griggs/Gurney p. 25 (top left); Griggs/REFLEJO p. 26 (bottom left), p. 32; Griggs/Harvey p. 28 (left); Griggs/Woldendorp p. 30 (left); Griggs/Englebert p. 31 (left); Robert Harding Associates p. 26 (top left), p. 28 (bottom right); Harding/Ian Griffiths p. 9 (bottom left); Alan Hutchison Library p. 13 (bottom left), p. 17 (top), p. 27 (bottom), p. 29 (bottom), p. 31 (top right); Hutchison/von Puttkamer p. 20 (top); Harding/Régent p. 30 (bottom right); Terry Jennings p. 9 (top left); Malaysian High Commission p. 23; Tony and Marion Morrison p. 9 (bottom left, top right), p. 14 (top), p. 15 (top right, bottom right), p. 18, p. 20 (left and right), p. 25 (right), p. 26 (top right), p. 33 (bottom right); Oxford Scientific Films/Bernard cover, p. 6, p. 7 (top right, bottom right); p. 10, OSF/Cooke p. 11 (top right), p. 13 (bottom right), p. 16 (center); OSF/Dalton p. 11 (bottom right), p. 12 (left); OSF/Fogden p. 8, p. 12 (right), p. 16 (top), p. 33 (left); OSF/Waina Cheng p. 13 (top left, top right); OSF/Survival Anglia p. 17 (middle); OSF/Survival Anglia/Lee Lyon p. 21 (left); OSF/Survival Anglia/Bartlett p. 25 (bottom left); OUP ©/Mark Mason p. 28 (inset); Ken Rubeli p. 24 (top and bottom); Jeffrey Tabberner p. 27 (top); Timber Research and Development Association p. 17 (bottom left, center right, bottom right); Zefa/Bonath p. 4; Zefa/Halin p. 15 (left); Zefa/Abril p. 29 (top); Zefa/Mohr p. 29 (center).

Illustrations by Norma Burgin, Stephen Cocking, Gary Hincks, Ben Manchipp, Ed McLachlan, Pinpoint Graphics, Tudor Art Studio, and Claire Wright.

# CONTENTS

# Tropical forests

All around the world, there are large areas of tropical forest. They are all near the Equator. The Equator is an imaginary line around the middle of the Earth. The temperatures are high all year long in some places near the Equator. The only time it gets cooler is at night. There is also a lot of rain all year round. Because of this, such forests are often called tropical rain forests.

The largest areas of tropical forest are in South America and West Africa. But there are some tropical forests in Indonesia, Malaysia, southern India, Sri Lanka, and Pakistan. Smaller areas occur in Australia and New Guinea.

Many useful things like rubber, Brazil nuts, bananas, coffee, cocoa, and nutmeg come from tropical forest regions. So do some of our most valuable timbers, such as teak, mahogany, and rosewood.

**A tropical forest in Hawaii**

**The tropical forests of the Earth**

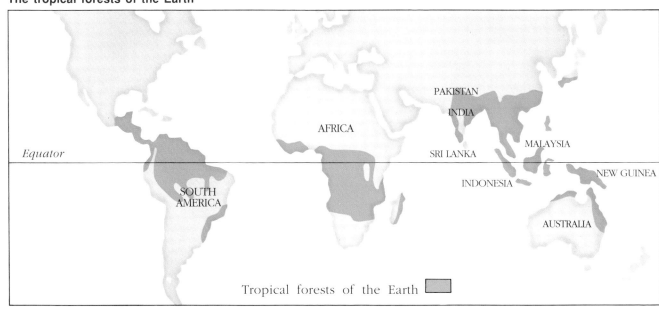

Tropical forests of the Earth

# Inside a tropical forest

Tropical forests are sometimes called jungles. This is not a good name to use because not all of these forests are dense. Often they are dense only at the edges or along the borders of rivers or clearings.

The inside of the forest is always dark because the trees keep their leaves all year round. So only a little light reaches the ground. Only a few ferns and other plants can grow under the trees. One big difference between tropical forests and forests in the rest of the world is in the huge variety of trees. For example, 2.5 acres (1 hectare) of temperate forest in Europe often contain only 10 to 12 kinds of trees. But 2.5 acres of tropical forest may have 200 kinds.

The trees in a tropical forest are also very large and close together. They are often 200 feet (60 m) high and have a circumference of more than 16 feet (5 m). Because the trees are evergreen, there are always leaves and fruits for animals to eat. So lots of animals, including birds and insects, live in tropical forests. All together, tropical forests are home for almost half of the different kinds of plants and animals in the world. There are so many kinds of plants and animals in tropical forests that many of them have not even been given names.

**Some of the many birds found in tropical forests — left: pied hornbill; top right: toucan; bottom right: vinaceous-breasted parrot**

# The parts of a tree

Trees are woody plants. They are the world's largest plants. All trees have three main parts. There is a thick woody stem called a trunk. Then there is the crown, made up of leaves and branches. There are also thin branches called twigs. During the year, buds, flowers, or fruit can appear on the twigs.

At the base of the tree are a large number of spreading roots. Some trees have one large root called a taproot. This taproot grows deep into the soil and has smaller roots growing from it. Other trees have many large and small roots. Roots often spread as far underground as the twigs spread overhead in the crown of the tree.

The roots anchor the tree. They stop strong winds from blowing the tree over. Roots also take up water and mineral salts from the soil. They take up huge amounts of water from the soil. In one day, the roots of a large tree may take up well over 50 gallons (200 l) of water from the soil.

**A tropical forest tree in Venezuela**

**The parts of a tree**

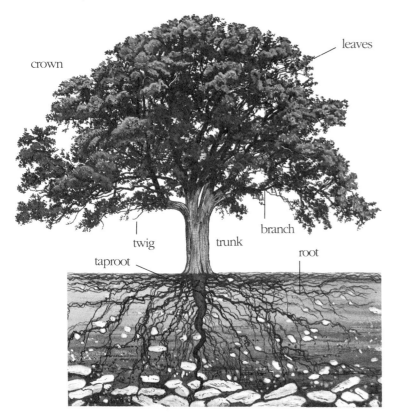

crown

leaves

twig

trunk

branch

root

taproot

# How a tree makes its food

The leaves make food for the tree. To make food, the leaves use the water and mineral salts that the roots take up from the soil. The water and mineral salts travel up the tree to little tubes in the veins of the leaves. Leaves also need sunshine and a gas from the air called carbon dioxide in order to make food. The green substance in tree leaves is called chlorophyll. Chlorophyll uses sunshine to turn the water, carbon dioxide, and mineral salts into food. One of the waste products of this process is oxygen. Most trees do not grow well in shady places because there is not enough sunlight for the leaves to make their food.

In many parts of the world, most trees lose their leaves in winter and grow new ones in spring. These are called deciduous trees. Common deciduous trees in North America are oak, ash, elm, and maple.

Some trees keep their leaves in winter. They are called evergreen trees. Spruce, pine, cedar, and yew are North American evergreen trees. Many trees in tropical forests are evergreens. The leaves of evergreen trees do not last forever. They fall off a few at a time throughout the year and are replaced gradually.

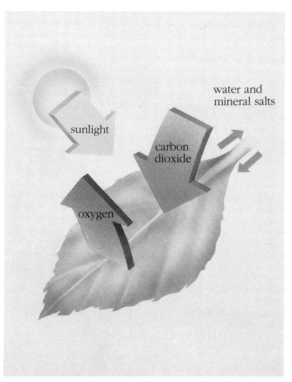

How leaves make food

Deciduous trees in summer and winter

# Death and decay

When leaves fall from a tree, they lie on the ground in the wind and rain. They gradually decay or rot away. Earthworms, millipedes, and other small animals eat pieces of the dead leaves. Tiny plants such as bacteria and fungi also break up the decaying leaves. Slowly, the leaves are changed to mineral salts in the soil. The mineral salts are used by plants to help make their food. The dead leaves act as natural fertilizers for the living plants. All kinds of plants, including trees, take up the mineral salts from the dead leaves. The salts then help them to grow.

When other parts of a tree fall, including the trunk, branches, and twigs, they too fall into decay. They also form mineral salts, which trees and other plants can use as food. The same mineral salts are being used over and over again.

In the cooler parts of the world, decay takes place slowly. Forests in cooler parts of the world often have a thick layer of dead leaves and branches on the ground. But in the hot, moist tropics, decay occurs quickly. And the leaves and branches that fall from the trees soon rot away. The mineral salts in a tropical forest are used over and over again very quickly.

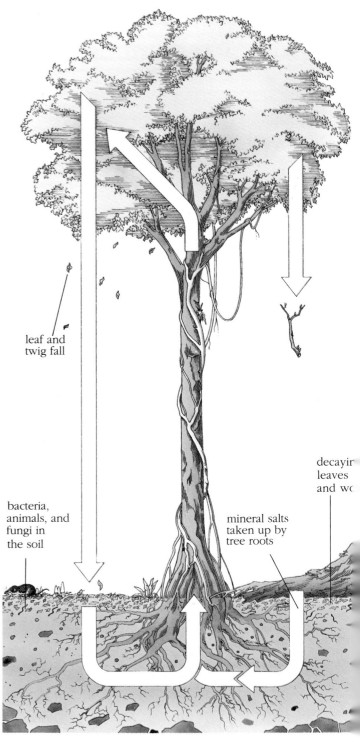

leaf and twig fall

bacteria, animals, and fungi in the soil

mineral salts taken up by tree roots

decaying leaves and wo

**A millipede feeding on dead leaves**

8

# Tropical forest trees

In the cooler parts of the world, winter is a difficult time for trees. The tree roots find it hard to get enough water. The trees stop growing. Often they lose their leaves and rest until the warmer weather returns. But in the tropical forests, the climate is warm and wet all year round. Most of the tropical forest trees are evergreens. Their leaves are dark green and tough. Each leaf usually has a drip tip. This lets the heavy rain run off the leaf. Tropical forest trees can grow and produce flowers and fruit all year round. Some have flowers and fruit six or more times a year.

The typical tropical forest tree is 130 feet (40 m) high. On most of the trunk, it has no branches. Branches begin to appear near the crown. The trees often have flowers growing straight out of the trunk or larger branches, instead of on twigs.

Many tropical forest trees have roots coming from the trunk above ground. These roots are called buttress roots. They act like the ropes on a tent and stop the tree from falling over. In swampy areas some of the trees have breathing roots. These roots grow above the wet ground and take in the air the tree needs to breathe.

Drip tip on a rubber plant leaf

Tree flowers growing from the trunk

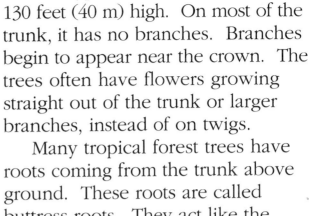

Tropical forest trees have large supporting roots

# The layers of the tropical forest

Tropical forests are built in layers. Here and there, huge trees stick up above the rest. Some reach 200 feet (60 m) or more in height.

The general level of the forest is made up of trees with rounded crowns. These are about 130 feet (40 m) high and have upright trunks. They are close enough for their crowns to overlap. Underneath these trees are layers of smaller trees and shrubs that make use of the little light they can get. Hardly any light reaches the ground. The forest floor is dark and damp. Mainly mosses and ferns grow there.

But other plants in the tropical forest grow at several levels. Woody climbing plants called lianes are rooted in the ground. They grow like huge ropes through the canopies of the trees. Having looped their way up one tree, the lianes grow through the crown to another nearby tree. The whole forest is tied together by these woody climbers.

**The five layers of a tropical forest**

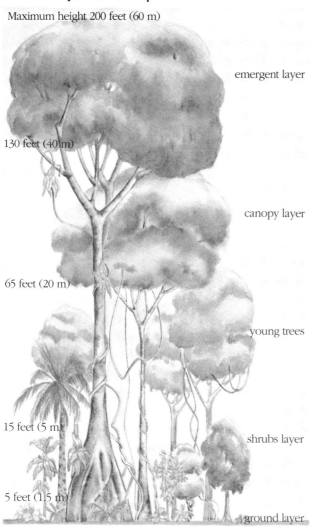

Maximum height 200 feet (60 m)

130 feet (40 m)

65 feet (20 m)

15 feet (5 m)

5 feet (1.5 m)

emergent layer

canopy layer

young trees

shrubs layer

ground layer

**Lianes in a Venezuelan tropical forest**

# Plants that depend on others

A typical forest tree has many plants besides lianes growing on it. Many of these are plants called epiphytes. Epiphytes need a lot of sunlight. They obtain it by growing high up on the branches of trees. These epiphytes do not use the tree for food. They merely use the tree to help them get enough sunlight. Among the epiphytes are beautiful orchids. Some of these have special roots to catch and store rainwater.

A few plants grow as parasites. They feed on the tree they are growing on. One parasite is the Malayan plant rafflesia. It has brilliant flowers and grows into the roots of lianes, feeding on their sap.

Above: a bromeliad epiphyte on a tropical tree
Left: a rafflesia flower
Below: fallen trees leave gaps in the forest canopy

At some point, each tropical forest tree has to die. When it falls, the tree will gradually rot away. Its remains will produce mineral salts that other plants can use. A fallen tree leaves a gap in the canopy of trees. Light can then pass through this gap and reach the ground. Some of the tree seeds on the floor of the forest grow. Soon a strong young tree grows and closes the gap.

11

# Animal life in the tropical forests

Tropical forests provide animals with food all year round. There are always flowers, fruits, leaves, and nuts for animals to eat. But much of this plant food is high in the trees. Birds are able to fly to reach their food. Many of them have developed special ways of getting their food. Toucans, for example, have long beaks. They use these to reach the fruits growing on thin branches. Hornbills have similar long beaks. Macaws and parrots have powerful beaks for cracking open nuts and fruit stones. Hummingbirds can hover while they sip the nectar from flowers with their long tongues.

Those animals that are not able to fly have to be able to climb to reach food. They are usually small and agile. They often have grasping fingers and a tail that can grip branches. Monkeys have fingers and tails like this. Tree snakes stay on branches by looping their bodies over them.

Few really large animals live in the forest because of the thick undergrowth. The animals that do live there do not have large horns or antlers that would catch on the trees. Most tropical forest deer are small. They run through the undergrowth using passages almost like tunnels.

**A hummingbird sipping nectar from a flower**

**Tree snakes live high above the forest floor**

# Invertebrate animals

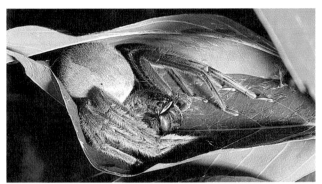

A bird-eating spider in its lair

A scorpion in a rainstorm

Tropical forest butterflies searching for moisture

Leaf-cutter ants at work

Invertebrate animals are those that do not have a skeleton of bone. There are many invertebrate animals in the tropical forests. They grow quickly in the warm conditions. The largest spiders live in holes and under fallen trees. Bird-eating spiders do this. These spiders can kill small birds with their poisonous jaws. Scorpions live on the forest floor. They use the sting at the end of their tail to protect themselves. They also use it to kill the small creatures they eat.

There are many large, beautiful butterflies and moths in the tropical forests. Most of them feed on the nectar from flowers. When they rest, some of these butterflies and moths look just like leaves. They are camouflaged. They are almost hidden, which protects them from being eaten by birds.

Thousands of kinds of ants live on the forest floor. Leaf-cutter ants climb trees and cut off pieces of leaves with their sharp jaws. The leaves are taken back to the ants' nest. There the pieces of leaves are made into little compost heaps. The ants feed on a fungus that grows on the rotting pieces of leaves.

# Forest soils

People used to think tropical forest soils were fertile. This was because so many large plants grew there. We now know that most of the soils in the tropical forests are poor. They are not very fertile. They give poor crops when the forest is cleared. This is because most of the mineral salts are in the trees. These trees stop the soil from being washed away by the heavy rain.

When the forests are burned down, for a time the ashes act as a fertilizer for the crops. But all the earthworms, termites, ants, bacteria, and fungi that turn the dead remains of plants into minerals are no longer needed, and they soon disappear. Soon the heavy rain washes away those mineral salts that are left in the soil. Few plants can then grow. And with no plants to protect the soil, the rain washes away the soil itself. So the area becomes barren. With no trees to soak up the heavy rain, the lower ground often floods. Farmers and loggers should try to take good care of the soil when they clear a tropical forest.

**The burning of tropical forest in Brazil**

**Forest clearance and consequent soil erosion**

14

# Mangrove swamps

In some places the tropical forests grow right down to the sea. Sometimes the trees can grow in the sea itself. The trees that do this are called mangroves. There are many different kinds of mangrove tree. They all grow where the water is shallow. Some mangroves are quite large trees, up to 100 feet (30 m) high. They are able to grow in the water because they have special breathing roots.

Mangrove trees also have unusual seeds. The seeds start to grow while they are still on the tree. When the seed has a long root growing from it, it falls from the tree and floats away. If it is washed up on the shore, the root sticks in the mud. The leaves are then able to grow from the seed above the level of the water.

Mangrove trees help build up the coast. Mud and pieces of dead plants collect in the tangled roots of the mangrove trees. Gradually the level of the mud is raised above the water. In time, new dry land is formed. Mangrove trees are homes for many wild creatures including otters, turtles, crabs, and some crocodiles and birds. They also provide firewood and cattle food.

**Roots growing from mangrove seeds**

**A mangrove swamp in Venezuela**

**A fiddler crab in a Colombian mangrove swamp**

# Survival in the forest

Tropical forests are difficult places for people to live in. They can be dangerous. In the swamps and rivers are crocodiles and alligators. There are poisonous snakes and scorpions. Many plants, too, are poisonous. Leeches drop from the trees onto people below. There are also leeches in the water. These will suck the blood of anyone they can attach themselves to.

Swarms of mosquitoes breed in the swamps and marshes. They carry deadly diseases such as malaria and yellow fever. When the Panama Canal was being dug through the swampy tropical forest of Central America, thousands of workers died. They died from malaria and yellow fever spread by mosquitoes.

But the native people who live in tropical forests know which plants they can eat. They know which snakes are poisonous. They also know which plants they can use to cure their illnesses or heal their

A poisonous frog in the South American tropical forest

A mosquito taking a meal of human blood

wounds. The native people are experts at living in these difficult and dangerous places.

American alligator

# Timber

Only a little of our timber comes from tropical forests even though these forests contain many valuable timber trees. One of the reasons loggers do not farm tropical forests is that the valuable trees do not all grow together. Mahogany trees, for example, are widely scattered in the forest. So the loggers' first problem is to find the tree.

Then it is difficult to cut down the trees. The base of the tree may have buttress roots growing around it. This means that the tree has to be cut where the trunk narrows above these roots. Often this is 10 feet (3 m) or more above the ground. Platforms have to be built so loggers have something to stand on to fell the trees. All the creepers and lianes may stop the cut tree from falling.

Moving the cut tree is another problem. Usually a rough roadway has to be built before the huge logs can be dragged out of the forest. Sometimes the trees can be floated away down a river. Unfortunately, many of the trees are too heavy to float. It is also difficult to find workers who will carry out this hard work in the hot, wet climate.

**Loggers building a platform around a tree**
**Carrying teak logs in India**

Mahogany

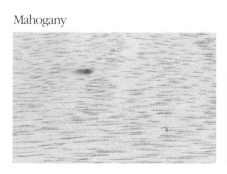

Teak

Iroko

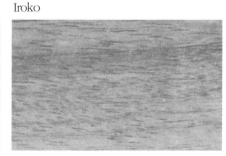

# The Amazon Forest

The Amazon Forest is in South America. It is the largest tropical forest in the world. It is roughly five times the size of Texas. The Amazon Forest covers a huge lowland area drained by the Amazon River and its tributaries.

Because the Amazon Forest lies across the Equator, the midday sun is overhead thoughout the year. The daytime temperatures are always high. The average temperature is 77°F (25°C). There is more than 78 inches (200 cm) of rain a year.

Each day in the forest is the same. The sun rises about 6 a.m. The early morning mists soon disappear. As the sun gets higher in the sky, the temperature rises. A lot of water evaporates from the rivers and also from the trees. As the warm, moist air rises, it cools. The invisible water vapor in the air cools to form huge clouds. By the afternoon, there is usually a heavy rainstorm,

**Rain clouds gathering over the Amazon Forest**

often with thunder and lightning. The clouds then break up. At about 6 p.m., the sun sets and the cooler night begins. There are no summer and winter seasons as we know them.

**The Amazon Forest and Equator**

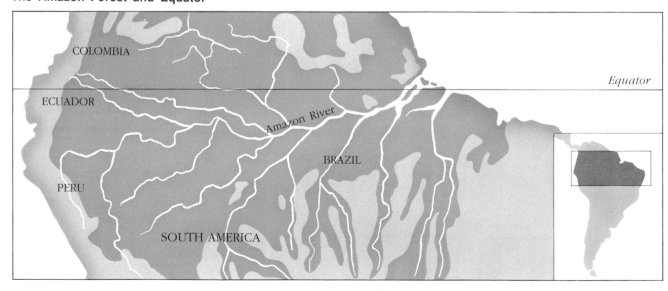

# Shifting cultivation

The Waura people live in the Amazon Forest. They are one of the tribes of Amazon Indians. The Waura get everything they need from the forest. They hunt animals with blowpipes and poisoned darts. They collect fruits and other parts of plants to eat from the forest. The Waura also carry out a simple kind of farming. This means they can live in one place for a long period.

In order to grow their crops, the Waura clear a space in the forest. At one side of the clearing, the Waura build large huts. These are made from wood and thatched with leaves. Each house is large enough to hold three or four families.

Crops grow quickly in the warm, moist ground. But only enough of the crop plants are harvested for each meal. It is impossible to store food in this hot, wet climate. In two or three years, the crops no longer grow well. The heavy rain has washed away the mineral salts from the soil. The Waura make a new clearing nearby in the forest. Eventually the clearing they are using is a long way from the village. Then the Waura must move to a new area. They make another clearing and build new homes. This kind of farming is called shifting cultivation.

**Waura man preparing his blowpipe**

**Clearing the trees and undergrowth to grow crops**

# The destruction of the Amazon Forest

**Making a road through the Amazon Forest**

In the past few years, over 6,000 miles (10,000 km) of road have been built through the Amazon Forest. This is so the forest can be cleared and used for other things. Large areas have been burned. Huge farms are taking the place of the forest. Millions of cattle graze the new land.

Tropical forest trees have been replaced by faster growing foreign trees. These are grown for wood pulp, which is used to make paper and rayon. Brazil's government has resettled over a million people from poorer areas. Many of them farm. Some grow food just for themselves, but others grow coffee, cacao, palm oil, and soybeans to sell. Some land is being cleared so oil and valuable minerals can be mined.

About one-fifth of the Amazon Forest has been cleared. At the present rate no trees will be left in 25 to 30 years. The Amazon Indians, animals, and birds will have no home. Environmentalists are worried — 50% of the Earth's oxygen comes from this forest.

**The farming of cattle on cleared rain forest land**

**Amazon Forest cleared for cultivation**

# The Congo forests

The largest tropical forest in Africa is the basin of the Congo River. This area was once a huge shallow lake. The Congo forests contain more kinds of plants and animals than any other parts of Africa do. This is the home of the gorilla, chimpanzee, and other kinds of apes and monkeys.

Bands of small people, or pygmies, live in parts of the forest. But much of the original forest has been cleared. Some has been cleared to obtain valuable timbers like mahogany and iroko. The less valuable timber is used locally for firewood or building. Some timber is made into plywood or chipboard. The trees are being cut down faster than new ones can grow.

Large areas of the forest have been cleared so landowners can plant huge fields of oil palm, rubber, bananas, and cotton. Some of the forest has been cleared to obtain oil

**The Congo in West Africa**

and minerals. Some has gone to make room for houses. Parts of the Congo have been set aside as national parks or nature preserves. But much of the forest is being threatened.

**A gorilla in the swamps**

**Chimpanzees**

# The smallest people in the world

A Bambuti tribal dance

In the tropical forests of the Congo live the smallest people in the world. These pygmy people are called the Bambuti. The average height of the men is 4 feet (1.3 m). The women are even smaller.

The Bambuti live in tribes made up of a few dozen people. They move through the forest, often following a herd of elephants or other animals that they hunt with spears and bows and arrows. At night the Bambuti make temporary shelters for their families. Thin sticks are stuck in the ground in the form of a circle. Then the ends of the sticks are bent over and tied in the middle. This frame is covered with large leaves to keep out the rain. The family's food is prepared and cooked outside the shelter.

The Bambuti have to exchange with nearby tribes for the other things they need, like salt and corn. They exchange ivory or honey from wild bees for the salt and corn. When they have finished working, the Bambuti enjoy music and dancing. In all, there are about 30,000 of these pygmy people in the Congo Basin. Once there were many more. It is believed that at one time these small people were found over much of Africa.

# The Negrito people of Malaysia

The Malay Peninsula is mountainous and covered by dense tropical forest. This forest is the home of the Negrito people. The Negritos are a race of small people. They live in family groups that can include up to 60 people.

The Negritos do not grow crops or keep animals. All their food and other needs come from the forest. They collect fruits, roots, nuts, and shoots to eat. The Negritos use snares and poisoned arrows to catch monkeys, rats, squirrels, lizards, and birds for meat. Fish are caught in the rivers with spears.

As soon as they have eaten all the food in one area, the Negritos move on to a new camp site. They sleep in caves, beneath rock overhangs, and in hollow trees. Sometimes they build raised shelters. Each of these is a framework of thin branches thatched with leaves. The only furniture is a wooden platform to sleep on. In less than a week, they leave camp and move on to a new one. They do not move just anywhere. Each tribe stays within its own territory, which covers an area of about 20 square miles (50 sq km).

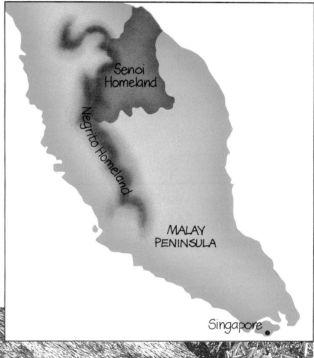

**A Negrito family**

# The Senoi people of Malaysia

Unlike the Negrito people, the Senoi of Malaysia are farmers. They live in a lonely mountainous area. Each group has a long bamboo house and several smaller huts.

Many Senoi carry out shifting cultivation. In the driest part of the year, they cut down and burn a small area of forest. The wood ash acts as a fertilizer. The Senoi then plant crops of bananas, rice, tapioca, and millet. They also fish and hunt using blowpipes and poison darts, and they collect wild fruits from the forest. The Senoi farmers do not have any food to sell. They produce just enough food to live on. After 2 or 3 years, the heavy rains have washed the mineral salts out of the soil. Then the people leave the clearing and make a new one.

**Below: a Senoi family**     **Right: Senoi children**

This kind of shifting cultivation works well as long as there are not too many people in the forest area. But there are more and more people in Malaysia. And the land is being taken over by wealthy farmers who want to grow crops to sell. These landowners are clearing large areas of land and planting rice and rubber trees. Soon there will not be enough land for shifting cultivation, and the Senoi will then have to start a new way of life.

# The Australian Tropical forests

Australia has only small patches of tropical forest left. The largest remaining areas are in the northeastern corner of Queensland. Parts of these have been set aside as nature preserves. These tropical forests contain many eucalyptus trees. Eucalyptus trees are often called gum trees. In the warm, wet forests, eucalyptus trees grow very tall. One kind can grow to be 328 feet (100 m) high. In the forests are some valuable timber trees.

Growing among the eucalyptus trees are strangler fig plants. Birds and flying foxes scatter the seeds of these plants. The seeds may lodge in the branches of a tree where they grow. The roots of the fig wind around the tree so much that the tree dies. The fig then grows in the

**Tropical forests in northeast Australia**

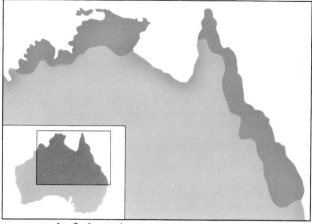

space left by the tree it has killed.

The Australian tropical forests are homes for several kinds of kangaroos and wallabies. Duck-billed platypuses live there, too. Where the forest has been cleared, farmers grow tropical fruits and sugar cane. These crops grow rapidly in the warm, moist climate. Some farmers keep cattle, also, for their meat and milk.

**A eucalyptus forest**

**A duck-billed platypus**

**A strangler fig**

# Plantations

In most parts of the world, large areas of tropical forest have been cleared to make way for huge farms. These farms are called plantations. Plantations grow tropical crops. There are many of these, including sugar, oil palm, cacao, coffee, rubber, bananas, pineapples, cotton, and rice. There are also a few plantations of timber trees such as teak. All of these crops are sold to countries overseas.

A lot of workers are needed on the plantations. Most of these workers have to be brought in from outside the forest areas. Special villages have to be built where the plantation workers can live. At one time, many of the plantation workers were slaves.

**Banana plant**

**Harvesting pineapples**

**Left: a pineapple plantation**

**Below left: an irrigation canal on a banana plantation**

Plants grown on plantations are no longer the same as those that grow wild. They have been changed by scientists. The banana plant, for example, no longer produces seeds. New banana plants are grown from pieces cut off the old plants.

A lot of fertilizers have to be used on the plantations. This is because the soil is poor. With vast areas being used to raise one crop, pests and diseases can spread quickly. Farmers use chemicals to kill the weeds and pests.

# Rubber trees

Natural rubber is made from latex. This milky white juice comes from the rubber tree. Rubber trees grow wild in the Amazon Forest. The rubber trees are widely scattered there. Because the trees are hard to find, it is expensive to collect enough latex to make rubber.

In 1876, rubber tree seeds were taken from South America to London. Little trees were grown from the seeds. These trees were sent to other countries with the same hot, wet climate as the Amazon Forest. Today plantations of rubber trees are grown in several countries. They can be found in Indonesia, Malaysia, Thailand, Sri Lanka, and parts of West Africa.

Today the rubber tree seeds are planted in special nurseries. As the seedlings grow, they are shaded from the hot sun. When they are large enough, the young trees are

Latex is the milky white juice obtained from rubber trees

planted out in rows. Other crops are planted between the rubber trees. These plants help keep the soil moist by shading it from the sun. They also help keep down the weeds and stop the soil from being washed or blown away. After about five years the rubber trees are 29 feet (9 m) high. They are ready to give the latex from which rubber is made.

A nursery of rubber tree seedlings in Nigeria

# Making rubber

The person who collects the latex is called a tapper. Work starts early in the morning. The tapper uses a sharp knife to make a sloping cut half-way around the tree. At the lower end of the cut, the tapper hangs a cup. Very slowly latex trickles from under the bark of the tree into the cup. Every two or three days, the tapper collects latex from each tree. One person may collect the latex from 300 to 500 trees in a day.

The latex is taken by truck to the factory. At the factory, acid is added to the latex. This separates the solid rubber from the liquid part. The rubber is rolled into flat sheets. When the sheets are dry, they are baled up and sent to those countries where rubber is used.

**Above: a rubber tapper at work**

**Below left: sheets of rubber hanging up to dry**

**Below: blocks of raw rubber    Inset:  rubber goods**

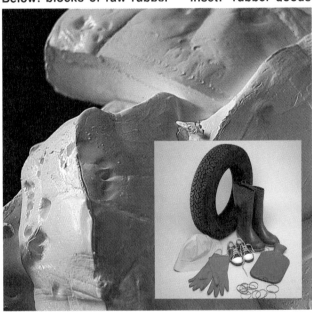

Rubber is used for tires, hot water bottles, boots, gym shoes, balls, hoses, and many other things. Today we use so much rubber that rubber trees cannot produce enough. A lot of rubber is now made from oil. For some things, this artificial or synthetic rubber is better than natural rubber.

# Cacao trees

Cacao trees have large seed pods. Each pod is about 10 inches (25 cm) long. Inside the pods are seeds called beans. It is from these beans that chocolate and cocoa are made.

Like rubber trees, cacao trees grow wild in the Amazon Forest. But now they are planted in other tropical areas. Mostly they are grown in Brazil and Ecuador in South America and in parts of West Africa. In South America, cacao is grown in large plantations. But in West Africa, it is grown on smaller plots. In West Africa, some of the taller trees are left when the forest is cleared. These shade the cacao trees. They also shelter the cacao trees from the strong winds.

The cacao trees begin to flower and bear pods when they are four to five years old. When the pods are ripe, they are cut off with a large knife. The pods are split open, and the cacao beans are scraped out. The beans are piled into heaps and covered with leaves. This is so that the pulp around the beans rots away. Then the beans are dried in the sun. When thoroughly dry, the beans are put into sacks and taken to the coast. Ships take the beans to Europe, America, and other countries where cocoa and chocolate are made.

**Top right: harvesting cacao pods in Brazil**

**Center right: cacao beans inside the pod**

**Bottom right: cacao beans drying
in the Nigerian sun**

# Oil palms

The oil palm tree grows wild in the tropical forests of West Africa. It is now grown in plantations in West Africa, Malaysia, and Indonesia. The oil palm grows tall and straight. It has no branches. But a mass of large, feathery leaves grows from the top.

The oil palm bears its bright, dried fruit in bunches. A bunch may weigh 30 to 45 pounds (15 to 20 kg). Because of the hot, wet climate, an oil palm tree grows quickly. It may flower and bear fruit between 12 and 20 times a year. A bunch is cut off with a sharp knife on the end of a long pole.

The fruits are taken to the factory where they are split open. Inside each fruit is a hard seed surrounded by a mass of fibrous tissues. Both the seeds and fibrous tissue contain oil. This oil is collected and used to make soap, margarine, and candles. Many people also use it for lights and for cooking.

**Bunches of oil palm fruits**

**Ripe fruits**

**Plantation of young oil palm trees**

# Coffee trees

Picking coffee in Colombia

Coffee berries from Kenya

Coffee beans being dried in the sun

Coffee trees came originally from Africa. Now plantations of them are grown in several places, including the tropical forest areas of Brazil and West Africa. The coffee trees are grown from seed in a nursery. After 18 months or so, the young trees are planted out in rows. Taller trees are planted between the coffee trees. This is to give the coffee trees the shade they need. Usually the coffee trees are grown on large plantations that contain thousands of trees.

When 4 years old, coffee trees produce small berries. As these turn cherry-red, workers pick them by hand. Inside each berry are two green seeds — the coffee beans.

To separate the beans from the fleshy parts of the berry, the berries are spread out on concrete floors painted black so they warm up in the sun. In a few days, the berries are dry and shrivelled, ready to be opened, sometimes by machine but mostly by hand. After being taken from the berries, the beans are then dried, sorted, packed in sacks, and shipped to the places where they are roasted.

# Sugar cane

Sugar cane is the main plant grown on the land cleared from tropical forests in the West Indies. It is also grown in Australia, Brazil, India, Cuba, and parts of the southern United States. Sugar cane is a very large member of the grass family. Some sugar cane plants grow to be over 20 feet (6 m) tall. The stems may be 2 inches (5 cm) in diameter at their bases.

Farmers living on plantations plant the sugar cane in the early spring. They do not replant it every year, for new plants will grow from the stalks of the old cane. Usually the cane is replanted every three or four years. The summer and autumn is spent keeping the sugar cane free from weeds. Only a few workers are needed for this job.

But the harvest is a busy time. In winter and spring, thousands of workers fill the cane fields. Sometimes cane fields are burned to drive off snakes and scorpions. The cane is cut by hand in many places. But machines are being used more and more. The cut cane is then quickly taken to the mill where it is cut into pieces. These are then crushed by huge rollers to squeeze out the juice. Finally, the juice is boiled until it forms crystals of sugar.

Cutting sugar cane in Brazil

# The disappearing forests

The world's tropical forests are in great danger. They are being cleared at a faster rate than ever before. In the time it takes you to read this sentence, people will have damaged or destroyed between 50-100 acres (20-40 hectares) of tropical forest.

They are clearing forests to produce timber, firewood, and food. They are clearing them to make room for factories, farms, houses, and roads. They are clearing parts of the forest to obtain oil and valuable minerals.

If people go on cutting down the forest at this rate, by the year 2000 only West Africa and the Amazon Basin will have any tropical forest left. People living in the forests will have lost their homes. Or they will have had to change their way of life. Some of the world's most interesting and beautiful plants and animals will have become extinct. Animals like the sloth, tiger, gorilla, orangutan, jaguar, and birds of paradise will have become extinct.

Trees purify the air we need

A bird of paradise

to breathe. The air in the forest changes if too many trees are chopped down. And this affects the weather. Some scientists are worried that if we cut down the big tropical forests, the world's climate may change.

A female three-toed sloth from Panama

A jaguar from Brazil

# Fact File

Here are some key facts about tropical forests that you will want to remember.

**1.** The tropical forests are all around the Earth at the Equator.

**2.** The tropical forests produce rubber, nuts, bananas, coffee, cacao, and nutmeg. They also produce timber — mahogany, teak, and rosewood.

**3.** Tropical forests are sometimes called jungles or rain forests.

**4.** There are many kinds of animals in a tropical forest because there is so much food there.

**5.** The three main parts of a tree are the crown, the trunk, and the roots.

**6.** Roots anchor a tree and draw up mineral salts and water to nourish it.

**7.** Food for the tree is made in the tree's leaves.

**8.** Most trees do not grow well in shade because leaves need sunshine to make food.

**9.** The parts of a tree that die and fall to the ground eventually decay into mineral salts.

**10.** Buttress roots come from the trunk above ground.

**11.** Lianes, or lianas, are woody climbing plants which grow in tropical forests.

**12.** Epiphytes are plants that depend on trees to reach sunlight.

**13.** A parasite feeds on the plant it grows on.

**14.** Many tropical plants have leaves with a drip tip to let the water run off.

**15.** An invertebrate animal has no bone skeleton.

**16.** Scorpions use their stings to protect themselves and to kill food.

**17.** People used to think tropical forest soils were fertile because large trees grew there.

**18.** When farmers burn down tropical forests for their fields, crops grow well for a year or two because the ashes act as fertilizer.

**19.** With no plants to protect the soil, the rainwater washes away the mineral salts.

**20.** A mangrove seed starts growing when it is still on the tree.

**21.** Mud and pieces of dead plants tangle in the mangrove roots. This helps to build up the river banks.

**22.** Leeches feed on people. Some feed on anything they can attach themselves to.

**23.** Mosquitoes spread malaria and yellow fever.

**24.** Alligators and poisonous frogs are just two of the dangerous animals found in jungles.

**25.** It is not practical to harvest from tropical forests because the trees are widely scattered and the buttress roots, creepers, and lianes interfere with cutting. Also, it is difficult to transport logs through the thick jungle.

**26.** The Amazon Forest is on the South American continent.

**27.** Sunrise in the Amazon is at 6:00 a.m. The morning is misty. Temperatures rise to 77° F (25° C). An afternoon thunderstorm is followed by sunset at 6:00 p.m. and a cool night.

**28.** Waura people use blowpipes and poisoned darts to hunt animals. They harvest and catch food for only one meal at a time because food spoils, so it cannot be stored.

**29.** Rubber trees are grown in Indonesia, Malaysia, Thailand, and Sri Lanka. The latex from the tree is made into rubber.

**30.** The Amazon Forest is being cleared to graze cattle, plant new types of trees, and grow new crops. About 20% has been cleared already.

**31.** Africa's largest tropical forest lies in the basin of the Congo River.

**32.** The Senoi people grow bananas, rice, tapioca, and millet.

**33.** The Eucalyptus tree is common in the tropical forests of Australia. So are kangaroos, wallabies, and the duck-billed platypus.

**34.** New banana plants are started from pieces cut off old plants.

**35.** Shifting cultivation means moving the crop as the land becomes infertile.

**36.** Cacao trees grow wild in the Amazon Forest. The seed pods are used to make chocolate and cocoa.

**37.** Palm oil is used to make margarine, soap, and candles.

**38.** Tall trees planted between rows of coffee trees provide shade.

**39.** Sugar cane is a grass plant.

**40.** Sugar cane is crushed with rollers to extract the juice. The juice is boiled and crystalizes into sugar.

# Further Research on Tropical Forests

The regions and climates of the world offer many chances to do further research. Many subjects are good for papers and reports. To research some subjects, you will find information you need in your library in books, magazines, and newspapers. Other subjects require you to interview people or to make your own observations. The topics and projects that follow are divided according to where and how you can get the necessary information. Pages 45-47 list books, addresses, magazines, and other sources of information that will be helpful for your work.

## Library Research

Following are some topics that are suited to research you can do in your library. You might want to write your research findings in a paper or keep a notebook for future work on the subject.

Though Earth is very old, scientific work on it continues. When you use library resources, be sure you note the dates of the books or other material. You will want the most recent information you can find.

Keep careful records of the title and author of works you use in your research. You may someday need to go back to them.

**1.** Look at a map of the world that shows the distribution of tropical forests. Roughly how far north or south of the Equator can a tropical forest occur? Why are there no tropical forests in East Africa or down the western side of South America, even in those places that are on the Equator?

**2.** Why are the temperatures near the Equator higher than those toward the polar regions? Why are the days all about the same length throughout the year?

**3.** The tropical forest areas receive more than 78 inches (200 cm) of rain a year. What is the wettest part of your country? Do tropical forests occur there?

**4.** Study your atlas. How many continents can you find that contain a large area of tropical forest? Name a country in each of these continents that contains a tropical forest.

**5.** Are the forests growing on mountains near the Equator similar to those growing on low-lying land?

**6.** Why do so few people live in the tropical forests?

**7.** At one time most of the workers on plantations were slaves. Find out where these slaves came from and how they were treated.

**8.** Why are rivers more likely to flood if forests growing nearby are cut down?

**9.** Mineral salts are vital to the growth of plants. In a tropical forest, most of the mineral salts are in the trees. They go into the soil only when the trees die. When farmers send crops to market, they are sending away mineral salts that would have gone into the soil if the crop plants had died and decayed where they were growing. How do farmers put mineral salts back into the soil to make up for those that have been lost?

**10.** Choose an animal that lives in one of the tropical forests. Find out all you can about it. How is it able to survive in the forest? Collect as many pictures as you can of your chosen animal. Make a book about your animal.

**11.** Draw or trace an outline map of the world. Shade in the areas of tropical forests. Mark in large rivers flowing through these forests. Find out more about these rivers.

**12.** A native in one of the tropical forests could probably get all the food he or she wanted with a bow and arrow. Yet a person from some-where else in the world would probably starve, even with a gun. Why do you think this would be?

**13.** One of the biggest dangers to the pygmies of the African tropical forests and to the Amazon Indians is disease. Hundreds of these people have died because they caught diseases such as colds, influenza, and measles brought to their part of the world by white people. Can you find out why these diseases should be so serious to the forest people when often they cause only mild illness in white people?

**14.** How do trees and other plants affect the air? In towns, why do people often plant trees along the sides of roads?

**15.** When tires and other things are being made from rubber, the rubber is usually vulcanized. What is vulcanization? Why is it done? Where has the name vulcanization come from?

**16.** What turns coffee beans from a green to a dark brown color?

**17.** Rice is an important food crop that is grown in several tropical forest areas. Find out where rice is grown and how it is looked after. How does the mud carried by rivers help rice to grow?

**18.** Find out more about the tropical forest animals that are in danger of becoming extinct. What, if anything, is being done to save these animals?

**19.** Through which of the countries of Africa with tropical forests does the Equator pass?

# Field Research

The topics and projects that follow require that you go outside books and other published sources for information. For some you need to watch what is going on around you in a systematic way. Plan carefully before you begin. Organize your materials. Keep clear and accurate records of everything that affects your findings. Be as careful and open-minded as possible. Don't let what you *expect* to find keep you from seeing something that is *unexpected*.

Some of these topics and projects require that you talk to people. Plan what you will ask. Be sure to make an appointment so you know you will be welcome. Explain to the person you are interviewing what you want to know and how you will use the information. This will help her or him help you.

## Topics and Experiments

The following experiments and topics are good for papers or reports. You won't be making anything, unless it is something that will help you illustrate your findings.

**1.** Places where collections of living plants are kept are called botanical gardens. If there is a botanical garden near where you live, visit it. What does it feel like to be in one of the greenhouses where gardeners grow tropical forest plants? What is done to make the conditions inside the greenhouse like that? What plants do gardeners place in tropical forest greenhouses?

**2.** Ants are almost everywhere. But they are particularly abundant in tropical forests. Find out what kinds of foods the ants in your garden or school ground like best.

Put a tiny piece of cracker or meat near the ants' nest. See how many ants come to the food. Do they pull the food to the nest? Now put down another piece of meat or cracker twice as big as the first piece. Do twice as many ants come to pull it into the nest?

Next put down four clean soda bottle caps near the ants' nest. Put a little jam in one, peanut butter in another, a little sugar in another, and a few bread crumbs in the last. Which cap do the ants go to first? Do they take the food to the nest?

Now try the experiment with other kinds of foods.

**3.** Find out about the content of soil. The soil in forests usually contains a lot of material called humus. Humus is the decaying remains of dead plants and animals. It is the humus in the soil that breaks down to form mineral salts.

To learn more about the content of soil, put a handful of garden soil in a jar with straight sides. Then pour in water until the jar is about three-quarters full.

Put the lid on the jar and shake it really hard. As soon as you have stopped shaking it, put the jar on a table or windowsill to see how the soil settles.

How long does it take for the water to clear? Can you see the layers of the different-sized pieces? How many layers can you see?

Which layer has the largest pieces? Which has the smallest pieces? Measure the thickness of each of the layers.

Are there any little pieces of humus floating on top of the water? These usually look black.

Do the same thing with soils from other places. Be sure you try a soil from under a large tree. If you always use the same kind of jar, you can make a table to compare the thicknesses and colors of the different layers in different soils.

**4.** How fast do leaves decay? Which tree leaves decay fastest? You will need some tree leaves of different kinds and some flower pots, yogurt pots, or margarine tubs containing moist garden soil.

Bury one leaf of each kind just under the surface of the soil in each pot. Label the pots with the names of the tree leaves in them. Put the pots on a warm windowsill and keep the soil moist. Every two weeks look at the leaves to see how much has decayed away. Then carefully bury

the leaves again. Do some of the leaves decay faster than others?

Put some more leaves in pots of soil. This time use leaves that are all of the same kind. Put some of the pots on a warm windowsill. Put the others in a cool place; a refrigerator would be ideal. Which leaves decay faster? Where would you expect tree leaves to decay faster, in the tropics or in the cooler parts of the world?

**5.** As we have seen, mosquitoes are feared in the tropical forests of the world because of the diseases they can carry. In the cooler parts of the world, gnats and mosquitoes do not carry diseases.

During the summer, look on the surface of still water for gnat or mosquito larvae. They are easily reared to adult insects in jam jars containing pond water, river water, or the stale water from a vase of flowers. Keep the jars outdoors.

Use a magnifying glass or hand lens to study the different stages in the life of a gnat or mosquito. Draw them in your notebook.

**6.** Where does the water go that a plant takes up? Get a potted plant — a geranium is ideal — or a young tree in a pot. Water the compost or soil in the pot. Then enclose the plant in a plastic bag with no holes in it. Tie the opening of the bag around the stem of the plant.

Stand the plant on a sunny windowsill. Look at the inside of the bag after a day or so. What do you see?

pencil you have uncovered seems to be the same height as your stick. Now see how many times that same piece of pencil goes into the height of the tree.

Suppose the piece of pencil goes into the tree 15 times; then your tree is 15 yards or meters high.

Use a tape measure or a piece of string and a ruler to measure how far it is around the trunk of the tree. This distance is called the girth, or circumference, of the tree.

Can you find a way to measure how far the branches spread in all directions without climbing the tree?

Which is the tallest tree you can find? How tall is it? Which tree has the biggest girth and the biggest spread of branches? How old do you think each tree is?

**7.** Measure the height of some trees. Find a stick that is one yard or meter long. Put that stick in the ground near the tree you wish to measure. Now stand far enough away so that you can see both the stick and the top of the tree.

Hold a pencil at arm's length, with its point toward the ground. Move your thumb until the piece of

**8.** Grow some tropical forest plants. Fig seeds are easy to grow. Scoop out the seeds from a dried fig and soak them in a cup of water to remove the sugary flesh. Spread the seeds on clean newspaper until they

are dry. Then sprinkle the dried seeds on the surface of a pot of moist potting soil. Cover the seeds thinly with some more soil. Stand the pot in a warm place until the first shoots appear. Then move the pot to a sunny windowsill. Keep the soil moist but not wet. Later, transplant the seedlings separately to small pots.

Peanuts or groundnuts are, in fact, not nuts but relatives of peas and beans. They need a good deal of warmth if they are to grow quickly and healthily. You can plant either shelled nuts or those still in their shells. Do not use roasted or salted nuts, though, and avoid any nuts that show signs of damage.

Plant the nuts in groups about 1 inch (3 cm) deep in a larger flower-pot that contains moist soil. Cover the pot with a plastic bag for two to three weeks. Once the nuts show signs of sprouting, move them to a

warm, sunny windowsill. Thin the seedlings out to about three or four to a large pot. Keep the soil moist but not soaking wet. You may not be able to get your peanut plants to produce ripe underground nuts, but they will soon grow into attractive house plants.

Other tropical and sub-tropical plants you might try to grow from seeds or beans include avocados, pomegranates, oranges, lemons, grapefruit, peaches, and coffee.

## Projects

The projects that follow help us understand conditions and principles, or natural laws, of tropical forests.

**1.** Make a collage. Collect pictures of tropical forest plants and animals. Stick your pictures on a large sheet of cardboard or poster board to make one large picture or collage that shows a variety of scenes in a tropical forest.

**2.** Learn which foods come from tropical forests. Many of the foods we buy in the grocery store are sold in cans, packets, bottles, or jars. The labels on them tell us what is inside the container and the name of the country where the food was grown.

Get a small map of the world and stick it in the center of a large sheet of poster board. Around the edges of the sheet, stick the labels of foods that were grown in tropical forest areas of the world. For each label, put a pin in the country it came from. Then join the label to the pin by a length of thread. Tape the end of the thread onto the label.

**3.** Make a collection of small pieces of the timbers produced in tropical forests. A carpenter might be able to help you get scraps of these. Label your collection. Try to find out what each of these timbers is used for. Why are these timbers better for these purposes than timbers from trees growing in other places?

**4.** Pineapples are grown in several tropical forest areas. It is possible to grow the spiky leaves on the top of a pineapple fruit as a potted plant. The best tops are fresh and green.

Cut off the tip, leaving about one-third inch (1 cm) of the fruit attached. Let it dry overnight. In the morning scrape away any flesh that is still soft and moist. Leave the central part untouched. Place it in a flowerpot containing moist potting soil or compost with a layer of pebbles on the bottom.

Cover the pineapple top and pot with a large plastic bag and put it on a warm, sunny windowsill. Remove the bag when new leaves appear in the center of the pineapple top.

Pineapple tops have produced fruit of their own. Even if yours should not do so, you will have an interesting and attractive plant.

**5.** A bottle garden imitates, in miniature, the warm, moist conditions in a tropical forest.

You will need a large bottle made of clear glass.

Put a layer of washed gravel about 2 inches (5 cm) deep in the bottom of the bottle. A cardboard tube and a large funnel will help

you get the gravel to the bottom of the bottle without dirtying the sides.

Next put in the bottle a layer of crushed charcoal about 2 inches (5 cm) deep. This helps keep the inside of the bottle clean and fresh.

Finally, carefully add a layer of potting compost or soil 4 inches (10 cm) deep.

Use a spoon or an old table fork tied to a stick to dig holes for your plants. Mosses and small ferns grow well in a bottle garden. So do ivies,

spider plants, and African violets. Place the taller plants in the middle or at the back of the bottle.

Pat the plants down with a thread spool attached to a stick.

Trickle water gently down the sides of the bottle. Do not stand the bottle in direct sunlight. Keep a top on the bottle, but take it off for a while if the inside of the bottle starts to cloud with condensation.

# Where to Go for Further Information

## Magazines

Here are some magazines for children that have articles about tropical forests. If your library doesn't have them, you can write to the publishers for information about subscribing.

*Dodo Dispatch*
34th Street and Girard
Philadelphia, PA 19104

*Elsa's Echo*
3201 Tepusquet Canyon
Santa Maria, CA 93454

*Owl*
The Young Naturalist Foundation
59 Front Street East
Toronto, Ontario
Canada M5E 1B3

*World*
National Geographic Society
Department 00487
17th and M Streets NW
Washington, DC 20036

*3-2-1 CONTACT*
P.O. Box 2933
Boulder, CO 80321

*TRACKS*
P.O. Box 30235
Lansing, MI 48909

*Ranger Rick*
National Wildlife Federation
1412 16th Street NW
Washington, DC 20036

## Addresses

The organizations and agencies below have information about tropical forests and related topics. When you write to them, tell them exactly what your subject is and what information you need. Tell them your name and address.

Friends of the Everglades
202 Park Street, #4
Miami Springs, FL 33166

RARE
c/o Winston and Strawn
255 M Street NW, Suite 500
Washington, DC 20037

International Society of Tropical
    Foresters
5400 Grosvenor Lane
Bethesda, MD 20814

Institute of Tropical Forestry
P.O. Box AQ
Rio Piedras, PR 00928

Organization for Tropical
    Studies, Inc.
P.O. Box DM, Duke Station
Durham, NC 27706

Hawaii Volcanoes National Park
Hawaii National Park, HI 96718

## Books

The following books are about tropical forests or have sections on the subject. You can find them in your library or bookstore. If you are not able to find them, someone at your bookstore may be able to order them for you.

*Animals of the Tropical Forests.* Johnson (Lerner)

*Closer Look at Jungles.* Pope (Watts)

*The Forest Book of the Jungle.* Hoke (Watts)

*Forests and Jungles.* Bains (Troll)

*Jungle.* Norden (Raintree)

*Jungles.* Catchpole (Dial)

*Jungles.* Podendorf (Childrens Press)

*Life in the Tropics.* Halsaert (Harvey House)

*Life of the Jungles.* Richards (McGraw-Hill)

*Rain Forests.* Eden (Merrimack)

*Trees.* Gordon (Troll)

*Tropical Rain Forests.* Goetz (Morrow)

## Places to Go

Here are some places where you can see tropical forests or plants and animals that live there. Some of these places have plants from forests, and some are located in forests.

Fairchild Tropical Garden
Miami, Florida

Hoo-Hoo International Forestry Museum
Gurdon, Arizona

Junior Museum of Bay County
Panama City, Florida

Mitchell Park Conservatory
Milwaukee, Wisconsin

Orchid Jungle
Homestead, Florida

Pacific Tropical Botanical Garden
Lawai, Hawaii

## Glossary

Here are the meanings of some words that you might have met for the first time in this book.

*Buttress roots:* roots that come from the trunk of a tree above ground. The buttress roots support a tree like the ropes on a tent.

*Chlorophyll:* the green substance that gives plants their coloring. Plants use chlorophyll to trap sunlight when making their food.

*Crown:* the part of a tree above the trunk. The crown is made up of branches, twigs, and leaves.

*Decay:* to rot away.

*Deciduous trees:* trees that lose their leaves in the autumn and grow new ones the following spring.

*Epiphyte:* a plant that grows on another plant and uses it for support in order to reach light.

*Evaporate:* when water is heated, it disappears into the air as water vapor. We say the water evaporates.

*Evergreen trees:* trees that lose their leaves a few at a time throughout the year.

*Fertile:* a good soil that is capable of growing many crops.

*Invertebrate animals:* animals that do not have a backbone inside their bodies. Most invertebrates are quite small.

*Jungle:* a term sometimes used for waste ground that is not cultivated. Sometimes tropical forests are called jungles.

*Latex:* the milky-white juice inside rubber trees from which rubber is made.

*Lianes or lianas:* woody climbing plants growing in tropical forests.

*Mineral salts:* the chemical substances that trees and other plants get from the soil and use as food.

*Parasites:* plants or animals that obtain their food by living inside or on other plants or animals.

*Plantations:* forests that have been planted by people to produce crops that are sold.

*Pygmies:* the name given to tribes of very small people.

*Rain forest:* another name for evergreen tropical forests that grow in wet places.

*Shifting cultivation:* clearing a piece of land, growing crops on it until the soil is no longer fertile, and then moving to new land.

*Timber:* the name given to the wood of a tree.

*Tropical forest:* a forest that grows near or on the Equator.

*Water vapor:* the invisible gas that forms when water is heated.

# INDEX